Trial Warrior's Book of Wisdom

A Compilation of Quotes for
Success in Law and Life

COMPILED & EDITED BY
MICHAEL S. WADDINGTON

Copyright © 2016 Michael S. Waddington

All rights reserved. This book or any portion thereof may not be reproduced or used in any manner whatsoever without the express written permission of the publisher except for the use of brief quotations in a book review.

Printed in the United States of America.

First printing, 2016.

Trial Warrior's Book of Wisdom: A Compilation of Quotes for Success in Law and Life

Michael Waddington
1018 Ashford Ave., Suite 3A-1
San Juan, PR 00907

Trial Warrior's Book of Wisdom/ Michael Waddington -- 1st ed.
ISBN-13: 978-1540746344

DEDICATION

To my little ninjas, Alexander and Emilia.

Books serve to show a man that those original thoughts of his aren't very new at all.

-Abraham Lincoln

INTRODUCTION

Throughout history, people have sought out the secrets to success, happiness, and health. From the Ancient Greeks and Chinese, to America's Founding Fathers, the wisdom needed to achieve success in all areas of life has been passed down through the ages. In this book, you'll find 2,500 years of wisdom at your fingertips.

There is a pattern in the passage of wisdom. The highest achievers have studied those who came before them. Socrates taught Plato, and Plato taught Aristotle. Aristotle went on to teach Alexander the Great. This cycle has continued through the ages. Some of our greatest thinkers and leaders—Benjamin Franklin, John F. Kennedy, Winston Churchill—studied ancient wisdom.

They understood such wisdom contained powerful lessons that could mean the difference between success and failure, happiness and despair, and life and death.

The path to wisdom is never-ending. To live a successful and fulfilling life, it is necessary to read and digest the knowledge of those who came before us, apply it to our daily lives, and pass it on to our loved ones. The effects of this practice are immense, and will permeate into all areas of life, both personal *and* professional.

Trial Warrior's Book of Wisdom

It is impossible to begin to learn that which one thinks one already knows.

-Epictetus

———————

Silence is one of the great arts of conversation.

-Marcus Tullius Cicero

———————

Associate with people who are likely to improve you.

-Seneca

As a man thinks in his heart, so is he.

-Solomon

If you are distressed by anything external, the pain is not due to the thing itself, but to your estimate of it; and this you have the power to revoke at any moment.

-Marcus Aurelius

Old minds are like old horses; you must exercise them if you wish to keep them in working order.

-John Adams

An investment in knowledge pays the best interest.

-Benjamin Franklin

Whether you think you can or can't, either way you're right.

-Henry Ford

Envy is a weed

that should not be watered.

-Cosimo de Medici

After considerable experience in coming into contact with wealthy and noted men, I have observed that those who have accomplished the greatest results are those who keep under the body; are those who never grow excited or lose self-control, but are always calm, self-possessed, patient, and polite.

-Booker T. Washington

To see the right and not to do it is cowardice.

-Confucius

Storms make the oak grow deeper roots.

-George Herbert

A friend to all is a friend to none.

-Aristotle

Where fear is, happiness is not.

—Seneca

Do nothing useless.

—The Book of Five Rings

It is better to deserve honors and not have them than to have them and not deserve them.

—Mark Twain

You may delay,
but time will not.

-Benjamin Franklin

The impediment to action advances action. What stands in the way becomes the way.

-Marcus Aurelius

A man convinced against his will, is of the same opinion still.

-Samuel Butler

Courage is resistance to fear,
mastery of fear,
not absence of fear.

-Mark Twain

It is the peculiar quality of a fool to
perceive the faults of others
and to forget his own.

-Marcus Tullius Cicero

If you're talking,
you're not listening.

-Anonymous

I have two doctors, my left leg and my right.

-G.M. Trevelyan

Love all, trust a few, do wrong to none.

-William Shakespeare

I never worry about action, but only inaction.

-Winston Churchill

There is only one way to happiness and that is to cease worrying about things which are beyond the power of our will.

-Epictetus

Better a little which is well done, than a great deal imperfectly.

-Plato

No man was ever wise by chance.

-Seneca

No man ever steps in the same river twice, for it's not the same river and he's not the same man.

-Heraclitus

Happiness depends upon ourselves.

-Aristotle

In conversation, humor is worth more than wit and easiness more than knowledge.

-George Herbert

First they came for the Socialists, and I did not speak out, because I was not a Socialist.

Then they came for the Trade Unionists, and I did not speak out, because I was not a Trade Unionist.

Then they came for the Jews, and I did not speak out, because I was not a Jew.

Then they came for me, and there was no one left to speak for me.

-Martin Niemölle

Lost time is never found again.

-Benjamin Franklin

You cannot escape the responsibility of tomorrow by evading it today.

-Abraham Lincoln

To find fault is easy; to do better may be difficult.

-Plutarch

What really frightens and dismays us is not external events themselves, but the way in which we think about them. It is not things that disturb us, but our interpretation of their significance.

-Epictetus

Do not impose on others what you yourself do not desire.

-Confucius

Travel is fatal to prejudice, bigotry, and narrow-mindedness, and many of our people need it sorely on these accounts.

Broad, wholesome, charitable views of men and things cannot be acquired by vegetating in one little corner of the earth all one's lifetime.

-Mark Twain

He that leith down with dogs shall rise up with fleas.

-Benjamin Franklin

If you know the enemy and know yourself, you need not fear the result of a hundred battles.

-Sun Tzu

Do not consider painful what is good for you.

-Euripides

Those who know how to win are much more numerous than those who know how to make proper use of their victories.

-Polybius

The happiness of a man in this life does not consist in the absence but in the mastery of his passions.

-Alfred Lord Tennyson

Physical fitness is not only one of the most important keys to a healthy body, it is the basis of dynamic and creative intellectual activity.

-John F. Kennedy

The mind that is anxious about future events is miserable.

-Seneca

Give me six hours to chop down a tree and I will spend the first four sharpening the axe.

-Abraham Lincoln

If you want to lift yourself up, lift up someone else.

-Booker T. Washington

The 80/20 rule states that, for many events, roughly 80 percent of the effects come from 20 percent of the causes. 20 percent of your effort will generate 80 percent of your results.

-The Pareto principle also known as the 80–20 rule

Delay is preferable to error.

-Thomas Jefferson

To put the world right in order, we must first put the nation in order; to put the nation in order, we must first put the family in order; to put the family in order, we must first cultivate our personal life; we must first set our hearts right.

-Confucius

A home without books is a body without soul.

-Marcus Tullius Cicero

Old age isn't so bad when you consider the alternatives.

-Marcus Porcius Cato

Great deeds are usually wrought at great risks.

-Herodotus

> I submit to you that if a man hasn't discovered something that he will die for, he isn't fit to live.

-Rev. Martin Luther King, Jr.

> Ninety-nine percent of the failures come from people who have the habit of making excuses.

-George Washington

Men naturally despise those who court them, but respect those who do not give way to them.

-Thucydides

To educate a man in mind and not in morals is to educate a menace to society.

-Theodore Roosevelt

Speech is the mirror of action.

-Solon

Often a very old man has no other proof of his long life than his age.

-Seneca

———————

Better three hours too soon than a minute too late.

-William Shakespeare

———————

It's better to keep your mouth shut and appear stupid than open it and remove all doubt.

-Mark Twain

Concentrate every minute like a Roman - like a man - on doing what's in front of you with precise and genuine seriousness, tenderly, willingly, with justice. And on freeing yourself from all other distractions. Yes, you can - if you do everything as if it were the last thing you were doing in your life, and stop being aimless, stop letting your emotions override what your mind tells you, stop being hypocritical, self-centered , irritable. You see how few things you have to do to live a satisfying and reverent life? If you can manage this, that's all even the gods can ask of you.

-Marcus Aurelius

To be wronged is nothing unless you continue to remember it.

-Confucius

The key is to keep company only with people who uplift you, whose presence calls forth your best.

-Epictetus

Don't look for more honor than your learning merits.

-Jewish Proverb

To keep the body in good health is a duty, otherwise we shall not be able to keep our mind strong and clear.

-The Buddha

Nearly all men can stand adversity, but if you want to test a man's character, give him power.

-Abraham Lincoln

When you have won a victory, tighten the strings of your helmet.

-Japanese proverb

One who is too insistent on his own views, finds few to agree with him.

-Lao Tzu

Faced with what is right, to leave it undone shows a lack of courage.

-Confucius

In skating over thin ice our safety is in our speed.

-Ralph Waldo Emerson

Difficulties strengthen the mind, as labor does the body.

-Seneca

Give every man thy ear, but few thy voice.

-William Shakespeare

Talk sense to a fool and he calls you foolish.

-Euripides

So other people hurt me? That's their problem. Their character and actions are not mine. What is done to me is ordained by nature and what I do by my own.

-Marcus Aurelius

Leave all the afternoon for exercise and recreation, which are as necessary as reading. I will rather say more necessary because health is worth more than learning.

-Thomas Jefferson

I've had a lot of worries in my life, most of which never happened.

-Mark Twain

Shooting fish in a barrel does not make you a marksman,
or a fisherman.

-William H. "Billy" Murphy, Jr., Esq.

Misfortune shows those who are not really friends.

-Aristotle

Some people are so afraid to die that they never begin to live.

-Henry van Dyke

No other offense has ever been visited with such severe penalties as seeking to help the oppressed.

-Clarence Darrow

Never argue with a fool, onlookers may not be able to tell the difference.

-Mark Twain

Many people take no care of their money till they come nearly to the end of it, and others do just the same with their time.

-Johann Wolfgang von Goethe

Wise men speak because they have something to say; Fools because they have to say something.

-Plato

The best defense is attack.

-Clausewitz

One man cannot hold another man down in the ditch without remaining down in the ditch with him.

-Booker T. Washington

Wealth consists not in having great possessions, but in having few wants.

-Epictetus

We are more often frightened than hurt; and we suffer more from imagination than from reality.

-Seneca

Me thinks that the moment my legs begin to move, my thoughts begin to flow.

-Henry David Thoreau

A liar needs a good memory.

-Quintillian

Run down the list of those who felt intense anger at something: the most famous, the most unfortunate, the most hated, the most whatever.

Where is all that now? Smoke, dust, legend…or not even a legend. Think of all the examples and how trivial the things we want so passionately are.

-Marcus Aurelius

The moment there is suspicion about a person's motives, everything he does becomes tainted.

-Mahatma Gandhi

Holding on to anger is like grasping a hot coal with the intent of throwing it at someone else; you are the one who gets burned.

-The Buddha

Little strokes fell great oaks.

-Benjamin Franklin

Though bitter, good medicine cures illness. Though it may hurt, loyal criticism will have beneficial effects.

-Sima Qian

Courage is being scared to death and saddling up anyway.

-John Wayne

Be polite to all,
but intimate with few.

-Thomas Jefferson

Don't expect to build up the weak by pulling down the strong.

-Calvin Coolidge

———————

Many of life's failures are people who did not realize how close they were to success when they gave up.

-Thomas Edison

———————

Pessimism never won any battle.

-Dwight D. Eisenhower

The beginning is the most important part of the work.

-Plato

Brevity is a great charm of eloquence.

-Marcus Tullius Cicero

My best friend is the man who in wishing me well wishes it for my sake.

-Aristotle

Power always thinks it has a great soul and vast views beyond the comprehension of the weak.

-John Adams

A bad beginning makes a bad ending.

-Euripides

First mend yourself, and then mend others.

-Jewish Proverb

Choose not to be harmed and you won't feel harmed. Don't feel harmed and you haven't been.

-Marcus Aurelius

The cautious seldom err.

-Confucius

First learn the meaning of what you say, and then speak.

-Epictetus

Move not unless you see an advantage; use not your troops unless there is something to be gained; fight not unless the position is critical.

-Sun Tzu

Short is the joy that guilty pleasure brings.

-Euripides

He who confers a favor should at once forget it, if he is not to show a sordid ungenerous spirit.

-Demosthenes

Luck is what happens when preparation meets opportunity.

-Seneca

———————

Success is not final, failure is not fatal: it is the courage to continue that counts.

-Winston Churchill

———————

By failing to prepare, you are preparing to fail.

-Benjamin Franklin

After I'm dead I'd rather have people ask why I have no monument than why I have one.

-Marcus Porcius Cato

Success is to be measured not so much by the position that one has reached in life as by the obstacles which he has overcome.

-Booker T. Washington

The right word may be effective, but no word was ever as effective as a rightly timed pause.

-Mark Twain

He who has a why to live can bear almost any how.

-Friedrich Nietzsche

Keep silence for the most part, and speak only when you must, and then briefly.

-Epictetus

> I learned that courage was not the absence of fear, but the triumph over it. The brave man is not he who does not feel afraid, but he who conquers that fear.
>
> -Nelson Mandela

> We are what we repeatedly do. Excellence then, is not an act, but a habit.
>
> -Aristotle

An ounce of practice is worth more than tons of preaching.

-Mahatma Gandhi

It is a rough road that leads to the heights of greatness.

-Seneca

Time is the wisest counselor of all.

-Pericles

Keep away from people who try to belittle your ambitions. Small people always do that, but the really great make you feel that you, too, can become great.

-Mark Twain

Moderation in all things.

-Terence

I am a part of all that I have met.

-Alfred Lord Tennyson

Sedentary people are apt to have sluggish minds. A sluggish mind is apt to be reflected in flabbiness of body and in a dullness of expression that invites no interest and gets none.

-Rose Fitzgerald Kennedy

One sword keeps another in the sheath.

-George Herbert

We are shaped by our thoughts.
We become what we think.

-The Buddha

Never leave that till tomorrow
which you can do today.

-Benjamin Franklin

The superior man acts before
he speaks, and afterwards
speaks according to his action.

-Confucius

He wins his battles by making no mistakes.

-Sun Tzu

An injured friend is the bitterest of foes.

-Thomas Jefferson

Criticism comes easier than craftsmanship.

-Zeuxis

Cling tooth and nail to the following rule: not to give in to adversity, never to trust prosperity and always take full note of fortune's habit of behaving just as she pleases, treating her as if she were actually going to do everything that is in her power.

-Marcus Aurelius

Neither borrower, nor lender be.

-William Shakespeare

To me, good health is more than just exercise and diet. It's really a point of view and a mental attitude you have about yourself.

-Albert Schweitzer

People are frugal in guarding their personal property; but as soon as it comes to squandering time they are most wasteful of the one thing in which it is right to be stingy.

-Seneca

He who talks more is sooner exhausted.

-Lao Tzu

To be ignorant of what occurred before you were born is to remain always a child.

-Marcus Tullius Cicero

Things may come to those who wait, but only the things left by those who hustle.

-Abraham Lincoln

As long as the world shall last, there will be wrongs, and if no man objected and no man rebelled, those wrongs would last forever.

-Clarence Darrow

When a judge compliments you, it usually means you have lost.

-James B. Donovan

Ignorance is the cause of fear.

-Seneca

Opportunity is missed by most people because it is dressed in overalls and looks like work.

-Thomas Edison

To get the full value of joy you must have someone to divide it with.

-Mark Twain

When you're finished changing, you're finished.

-Benjamin Franklin

Fear is only as deep as the mind allows.

-Japanese Proverb

Emotional decisions are usually bad decisions.

-Anonymous

Education is the most powerful weapon you can use to change the world.

-Nelson Mandela

If the body be feeble, the mind will not be strong. The sovereign invigorator of the body is exercise, and of all the exercises walking is best.
I have known some great walkers and had particular accounts of many more; and I never knew or heard of one who was not healthy and long lived.

-Thomas Jefferson

If you tell the truth, you don't have to remember anything.

-Mark Twain

It's easier to do a job right than to explain why you didn't.

-Martin Van Buren

Success is how high you bounce when you hit bottom.

-George S. Patton

The first man gets the oyster, the second man gets the shell.

-Andrew Carnegie

Courage is knowing what not to fear.

-Plato

I count him braver who overcomes his desires than him who conquers his enemies, for the hardest victory is over the self.

-Aristotle

He who is brave is free.

-Seneca

Our minds are like our stomachs; they are whetted by the change of their food, and variety supplies both with fresh appetites.

-Marcus Fabius Quintilian

You see a louse on someone else, but not a tick on yourself.

-Gaius Petronius Arbiter

Absence makes the heart grow fonder.

-Propertius Sextus

The first virtue is to restrain the tongue; he approaches nearest to the gods who knows how to be silent, even though he is in the right.

-Marcus Porcius Cato

Small opportunities are often the beginning of great enterprises.

-Demosthenes

Haste in every business brings failures.

-Herodotus

When you first rise in the morning tell yourself: I will encounter busybodies, ingrates, egomaniacs, liars, envy-mongers, and cranks. They are all stricken with these afflictions because they don't know the difference between good and evil. Because I have understood the beauty of good and the ugliness of evil, I know that these wrong-doers are still akin to me, and that none can do me harm, or implicate me in ugliness.

-Marcus Aurelius

Never let grass grow under your feet.

—Jewish Proverb

When in doubt, don't.

—Benjamin Franklin

The readiest and surest way to get rid of censure, is to correct ourselves.

—Demosthenes

By three methods we may learn: First, by reflection, which is noblest; Second, by imitation, which is easiest; and third by experience, which is the bitterest.

-Confucius

In war, the way is to avoid what is strong and to strike at what is weak.

-Sun Tzu

We have two ears and one mouth so that we can listen twice as much as we speak.

-Epictetus

Cowards die many times before their deaths; the valiant never taste of death but once.

-William Shakespeare

There are three faithful friends, and old wife, an old dog, and ready money.

-Benjamin Franklin

> A friend is one who has the same enemies as you have.

-Abraham Lincoln

> When I was a boy of 14, my father was so ignorant I could hardly stand to have the old man around.
>
> But when I got to be 21, I was astonished at how much the old man had learned in seven years.

-Mark Twain

Liberty cannot be preserved without general knowledge among the people.

-John Adams

Health and cheerfulness naturally beget each other.

-Joseph Addison

Choose a job you love, and you will never have to work a day in your life.

-Confucius

> What power has law where only money rules.
>
> -Gaius Petronius Arbiter

> As circumstances are favorable, one should modify one's plans.
>
> -Sun Tzu

> The bravest are surely those who have the clearest vision of what is before them, glory and danger alike, and yet notwithstanding, go out to meet it.
>
> -Thucydides

Nothing can stop the man with the right mental attitude from achieving his goal; nothing on earth can help the man with the wrong mental attitude.

- Thomas Jefferson

Courtesy is as much a mark of a gentleman as courage.

-Theodore Roosevelt

When marrying, ask yourself this question: Do you believe that you will be able to converse well with this person into your old age? Everything else in marriage is transitory.

-Friedrich Nietzsche

If it don't seem like it's worth the effort, it probably ain't.

-Anonymous

Acquaintance lessens fame.

-Claudius

Take calculated risks. That is quite different from being rash.

- George S. Patton

Facts are stubborn things; and whatever may be our wishes, our inclinations, or the dictates of our passion, they cannot alter the state of facts and evidence.

-John Adams

The foolish and the dead alone never change their opinion.

-James Russell Lowell

A multitude of words is no proof of a prudent mind.

-Thales

Until we have begun to go without them, we fail to realize how unnecessary many things are. We've been using them not because we needed them but because we had them.

-Seneca

What you leave behind is not what is engraved in stone monuments, but what is woven into the lives of others.

-Pericles

To remind a man of a kindness conferred and to talk of it, is little different from reproach.

-Demosthenes

Ignorance is the root and stem of all evil.

-Plato

If you add a little to a little, and then do it again, soon that little shall be much.

-Hesiod

Never give in, never give in, never, never, never, never - in nothing, great or small, large or petty - never give in except to convictions of honor and good sense.

-Winston Churchill

Rapidity is the essence of war: take advantage of the enemy's unreadiness, make your way by unexpected routes, and attack unguarded spots.

-Sun Tzu

Your very silence shows you agree.

-Euripides

Everything has its beauty but not everyone sees it.

-Confucius

Tact is the ability to describe others as they see themselves.

-Abraham Lincoln

Nothing builds self-esteem and self-confidence like accomplishment.

-Thomas Carlyle

Things do not happen. Things are made to happen.

-John F. Kennedy

There are two sides to every question.

-Protagoras

Be a craftsman in speech that thou mayest be strong, for the strength of one is the tongue, and speech is mightier than all fighting.

-Maxims of Ptahhotep

The time to repair the roof is when the sun is shining.

- John F. Kennedy

A man's character is his fate.

-Heraclitus

Never argue with stupid people, they will drag you down to their level and then beat you with experience.

-Mark Twain

If you find yourself in a hole, the first thing to do is stop diggin'.

-Anonymous

Nothing is easier than self-deceit. For what each man wishes, that he also believes to be true.

-Demosthenes

Use your health, even to the point of wearing it out. That is what it is for. Spend all you have before you die; do not outlive yourself.

-Bernard Shaw

He who knows that enough is enough will always have enough.

-Lao Tzu

It is the mark of an educated mind to be able to entertain a thought without accepting it.

-Aristotle

———————

A pessimist sees the difficulty in every opportunity;
an optimist sees the opportunity in every difficulty.

-Winston Churchill

Respond intelligently even to unintelligent treatment.

-Lao Tzu

In matters of style, swim with the current; in matters of principle, stand like a rock.

-Thomas Jefferson

Live as if you were to die tomorrow. Learn as if you were to live forever.

-Mahatma Gandhi

Keep your eyes wide open before marriage, half shut afterwards.

-Benjamin Franklin

Be careful to leave your sons well instructed rather than rich, for the hopes of the instructed are better than the wealth of the ignorant.

-Epictetus

Wrinkles should merely indicate where the smiles have been.

-Mark Twain

Without health, life is not life;
it is only a state of languor
and suffering.

-Francois Rabelais

If you're ridin' ahead of the herd, take a look back every now and then to make sure it's still there with ya.

-Anonymous

Everything has beauty,
but not everyone sees it.

-Confucius

Nature does not hurry, yet everything is accomplished.

-Lao Tzu

It is neither wealth nor splendor; but tranquility and occupation which give you happiness.

-Thomas Jefferson

Suspicion always haunts the guilty mind.

-William Shakespeare

No man has a good enough memory to be a successful liar.

-Abraham Lincoln

Those who cannot understand how to put their thoughts on ice should not enter into the heat of debate.

-Friedrich Nietzsche

When you give a personal lesson in meanness to a critter or to a person, don't be surprised if they learn their lesson.

-Anonymous

Let us never negotiate out of fear. But let us never fear to negotiate.

-John F. Kennedy

When you see a rattlesnake poised to strike you, do not wait until he has struck before you crush him.

-Franklin D. Roosevelt

No man ever listened himself out of a job.

-Calvin Coolidge

Success depends upon previous preparation, and without such preparation there is sure to be failure.

-Confucius

Any man can make mistakes, but only an idiot persists in his error.

-Marcus Tullius Cicero

No one loves the man whom he fears.

-Aristotle

He who knows, does not speak.
He who speaks, does not know.

-Lao Tzu

Injustice anywhere is a threat to justice everywhere.

-Rev. Martin Luther King, Jr.

Let no one be willing to speak ill of the absent.

-Propertius Sextus

Anger, if not restrained, is frequently more hurtful to us than the injury that provokes it.

-Seneca

Twenty years from now you will be more disappointed by the things that you didn't do than by the ones you did do.

-Mark Twain

Well done is better than well said.

-Benjamin Franklin

Nothing in this world can take the place of persistence. Talent will not; nothing is more common than unsuccessful men with talent. Genius will not; unrewarded genius is almost a proverb. Education will not; the world is full of educated derelicts. Persistence and determination alone are omnipotent. The slogan Press On! has solved and always will solve the problems of the human race.

-Calvin Coolidge

He who commits injustice is ever made more wretched than he who suffers it.

-Plato

Three things cannot be long hidden: the sun, the moon, and the truth.

-The Buddha

Stay alert, stay alive.

-Army saying

Liars when they speak the truth are not believed.

-Aristotle

Waste not fresh tears over old griefs.

-Euripides

Better be wise by the misfortunes of others than by your own.

-Aesop

Advice is judged by results, not by intentions.

-Cicero

When the mind is thinking, it is talking to itself.

-Plato

To secure ourselves against defeat lies in our own hands, but the opportunity of defeating the enemy is provided by the enemy himself.

-Sun Tzu

If you're going through hell, keep going.

-Winston Churchill

One father is more than a hundred schoolmasters.

-George Herbert

Say not always what you know, but always know what you say.

-Claudius

True happiness is to enjoy the present, without anxious dependence upon the future, not to amuse ourselves with either hopes or fears but to rest satisfied with what we have, which is sufficient, for he that is so wants nothing. The greatest blessings of mankind are within us and within our reach. A wise man is content with his lot, whatever it may be, without wishing for what he has not.

–Seneca

Wisely, and slow.

They stumble that run fast.

-William Shakespeare

To know what you know and what you do not know, that is true knowledge.

-Confucius

You have enemies? Good. That means you've stood up for something, sometime in your life.

-Winston Churchill

An early-morning walk is a blessing for the whole day.

-Henry David Thoreau

The most important part of education is proper training in the nursery.

-Plato

Men acquire a particular quality by constantly acting in a particular way.

-Aristotle

The difference between the almost right word and the right word is really a large matter. 'tis the difference between the lightning bug and the lightning.

-Mark Twain

The moment a person forms a theory, his imagination sees in every object only the traits which favor that theory.

-Thomas Jefferson

Beware the barrenness of a busy life.

-Socrates

He who acts with a constant view to his own advantage will be much murmured against.

-Confucius

Who you choose to marry will be the most import decision in your life. It will affect your health, your wealth, and your happiness and that of your offspring.

-Anonymous

It is of great importance to set a resolution, not to be shaken, never to tell an untruth. There is no vice so mean, so pitiful, so contemptible; and he who permits himself to tell a lie once, finds it much easier to do it a second and third time, till at length it becomes habitual; he tells lies without attending to it, and truths without the world's believing him. This falsehood of the tongue leads to that of the heart, and in time depraves all its good dispositions.

-Thomas Jefferson

As you teach, you learn.

-Jewish Proverb

Keep thy shop and thy shop will keep thee.

-Benjamin Franklin

A man reaps what he sows.

-Galatians 6:7

Nothing is more terrible than ignorance in action.

- Johann Wolfgang von Goethe

The leading rule for the lawyer, as for the man of every calling, is diligence.

-Abraham Lincoln

We learn not in the school, but in life.

-Seneca

It is health that is real wealth and not pieces of gold and silver.

-Mahatma Gandhi

It is in times of security that the spirit should be preparing itself for difficult times; while fortune is bestowing favors... is the time for it to be strengthened against her rebuffs.

-Seneca

The more man meditates upon good thoughts, the better will be his world and the world at large.

-Confucius

The greater the difficulty, the greater the glory.

-Marcus Tullius Cicero

When angry, count to ten before you speak. If very angry, count to one hundred.

-Thomas Jefferson

Pleasure in the job puts perfection in the work.

-Aristotle

I hear and I forget. I see and I remember. I do and I understand.

-Confucius

Most folks are as happy as they make up their minds to be.

-Abraham Lincoln

> There is no harm in repeating a good thing.
>
> -Plato

> Always acknowledge a fault. This will throw those in authority off their guard and give you an opportunity to commit more.
>
> -Mark Twain

> When the well's dry, we know the worth of water.
>
> -Benjamin Franklin

At dawn, when you have trouble getting out of bed, tell yourself: "I have to go to work-as a human being. What do I have to complain of, if I'm going to do what I was born for-the things which I was brought into the world to do? Or is this what I was created for? To huddle under the blankets and stay warm?" -But it's nicer here…So you were born to feel "nice?" Instead of doing things and experiencing them? Why aren't you running to do what your nature demands? But we have to sleep sometime…Agreed. But nature set a limit on that-as it did on eating and drinking. And you're over the limit. But not of working. There you're still below your quota. You don't love yourself enough. Or you'd love your nature too and what it demands of you.

-Marcus Aurelius

No act of kindness, no matter how small, is ever wasted.

-Aesop

To fight and conquer in all your battles is not supreme excellence; supreme excellence consists in breaking the enemy's resistance without fighting.

-Sun Tzu

Know how to listen and you will profit even from those who talk badly.

-Epictetus

He who does not condemn evil commands it to be done.

-Leonardo da Vinci

I have found out that there ain't no surer way to find out whether you like people or hate them than to travel with them.

-Mark Twain

Health and intellect are the two blessings of life.

-Menander

> Courage is what it takes to stand up and speak; courage is also what it takes to sit down and listen.
>
> -Winston Churchill

> Energy and persistence conquer all things.
>
> -Benjamin Franklin

> People ask for your criticism, but they only want your praise.
>
> -W. Somerset Maugham

If a man neglects education, he walks lame to the end of his life.

–Plato

To do nothing evil is good;
to wish nothing evil is better.

-Claudius

Put more trust in nobility of character than in an oath.

-Solon

Dost thou love life? Then do not squander time, for that is the stuff life is made of.

-Benjamin Franklin

Wealth consists not in having great possessions, but in having few wants.

-Epictetus

Better to remain silent and be thought a fool than to speak out and remove all doubt.

-Abraham Lincoln

Always be friendlier than necessary. Always be kinder than necessary. Always be more generous than necessary.

-Anonymous

You cannot parcel out freedom in pieces because freedom is all or nothing.

-Tertullian

Deceive not thy physician, confessor, nor lawyer.

-George Herbert

In giving advice seek to help, not to please, your friend.

-Solon

Day by day, what you choose, what you think and what you do is who you become.

-Heraclitus

It is said that famous men are usually the product of unhappy childhood. The stern compression of circumstances, the twinges of adversity, the spur of slights and taunts in early years, are needed to evoke that ruthless fixity of purpose and tenacious mother without which great actions are seldom accomplished.

-Winston Churchill

If a man knows not to which port he sails, no wind is favorable.

-Seneca

It's easy to make friends, but hard to get rid of them.

-Mark Twain

Walking is the best possible exercise. Habituate yourself to walk very far.

-Thomas Jefferson

The only man who never makes a mistake is the man who never does anything.

-Theodore Roosevelt

The true measure of a man is how he treats someone who can do him absolutely no good.

-Samuel Johnson King

A goal without a plan is just a wish.

-Antoine de Saint-Exupery

He who lives only to benefit himself confers on the world a benefit when he dies.

-Tertullian

The secret of happiness is freedom. The secret of freedom is courage.

-Thucydides

We must hang together... or we shall most assuredly hang separately.

-Benjamin Franklin

What is harder than rock? What is softer than water? Yet hard rocks are hollowed out by soft water?

-Seneca

There was never a genius without a tincture of madness.

-Aristotle

Grief walks upon the heels of pleasure; married in haste, we repent at leisure.

-William Congreve

Determine never to be idle. No person will have occasion to complain of the want of time who never loses any. It is wonderful how much may be done if we are always doing.

-Thomas Jefferson

You must lose a fly to catch a trout.

-George Herbert

Practice yourself for heaven's sake, in little things; and thence proceed to greater.
-Epictetus

One should learn even from one's enemies.
-Ovid

Your life is an expression of all your thoughts.
-Marcus Aurelius

However beautiful the strategy, you should occasionally look at the results.

-Winston Churchill

Alexander the Great and his mule driver both died, and the same thing happened to both.

-Marcus Aurelius

Nobody loves life like an old man.

-Sophocles

Speak the truth, do not yield to anger; give, if thou art asked for little; by these three steps thou wilt go near the gods.

-Confucius

The pretended admission of a fault on our part creates an excellent impression.

-Marcus Fabius Quintilian

Afflicted by love's madness all are blind.

-Propertius Sextus

The greatest wealth is health.

-Virgil

Do not bite the bait of pleasure till you know there is no hook beneath it.

-Thomas Jefferson

We are all born ignorant, but one must work hard to remain stupid.

-Benjamin Franklin

Never interrupt your enemy when he is making a mistake.

-Napoleon Bonaparte

The only truth is in knowing you know nothing.

-Socrates

Don't fight anyone that has nothing to lose.

-Anonymous

You live as if you were destined to live forever, no thought of your frailty ever enters your head, of how much time has already gone by you take no heed. You squander time as if you drew from a full and abundant supply, though all the while that day which you bestow on some person or thing is perhaps your last.

-Seneca

Excuses sound best to the person that's making them up.

-Anonymous

The falling drops at last will wear the stone.

-Lucretius

Force has no place where there is need of skill.

-Herodotus

Let every eye negotiate for itself and trust no agent.

-William Shakespeare

What such a man needs is not courage but nerve control, cool headedness. This he can only get by practice.

-Theodore Roosevelt

Be content with what you have; rejoice in the way things are. When you realize there is nothing lacking, the whole world belongs to you.

-Lao Tzu

We are what we repeatedly do. Excellence, then, is not an act but a habit.

-Aristotle

When it is obvious that the goals cannot be reached, don't adjust the goals, adjust the action steps.

-Confucius

The best measure of the quality of a society is the quality of its justice.

-Winston Churchill

Anger is an acid that can do more harm to the vessel in which it is stored than to anything on which it is poured.

-Mark Twain

All truly great thoughts are conceived while walking.

-Friedrich Nietzsche

The roots of education are bitter, but the fruit is sweet.

–Aristotle

When your opponent's sittin' there holding all aces, there's only one thing left to do: Kick over the table.

-Dean Martin

Better never begin than never make an end.

-George Herbert

Be amusing: never tell unkind stories; above all, never tell long ones.

-Benjamin Disraeli

> What we are is what we have thought for years.
>
> -The Buddha

> There is no witness so dreadful, no accuser so terrible as the conscience that dwells in the heart of every man.
>
> -Polybius

> All warfare is based on deception.
>
> -Sun Tzu

He is a wise man who does not grieve for the things which he has not, but rejoices for those which he has.

-Epictetus

Let each man pass his days in that wherein his skill is greatest.

-Propertius Sextus

They can do all because they think they can.

-Virgil

It does not matter how slowly you go as long as you do not stop.

-Confucius

Early to bed and early to rise makes a man healthy, wealthy, and wise.

-Benjamin Franklin

The human race has only one really effective weapon and that is laughter.

-Mark Twain

How much pain they have cost us, the evils which have never happened.

-Thomas Jefferson

Practice yourself, for heaven's sake in little things, and then proceed to greater.

-Epictetus

Courage is the most important attribute of a lawyer.

-Robert F. Kennedy

Familiarity breeds contempt,
while rarity wins admiration.

-Apuleius

How far you go in life depends on your being tender with the young, compassionate with the aged, sympathetic with the striving, and tolerant of the weak and strong; because some day in your life, you will have been all of those.

-George Washington Carver

We live in deeds, not years; in thoughts, not breaths; in feelings, not in figures on a dial. We should count time by heart throbs. He most lives who thinks most, feels the noblest, acts the best.

-Aristotle

It is not the man who has too little, but the man who craves more, that is poor.

-Seneca

Where there is love there is life.

-Mahatma Gandhi

The wrongdoer is more unfortunate
than the man wrongbeld.

-Democritus

A superior man is modest in his speech, but exceeds in his actions.

-Confucius

Justice has nothing to do with what goes on in a courtroom; Justice is what comes out of a courtroom.

-Clarence Darrow

False words are not only evil in themselves, but they infect the soul with evil.

-Socrates

One travels more usefully when alone, because he reflects more.

-Thomas Jefferson

I am prepared for the worst, but hope for the best.

-Benjamin Disraeli

Life is like a play: it's not the length, but the excellence of the acting that matters.

-Seneca

Courage is of no value unless accompanied by justice; yet if all men became just, there would be no need for courage.

-Agesilaus the Second

Success consists of going from failure to failure without loss of enthusiasm.

-Winston Churchill

A lean compromise is better than a fat lawsuit.

-George Herbert

Good habits formed at youth make all the difference.

-Aristotle

Don't let your imagination be crushed by life as a whole. Don't try to picture everything bad that could possibly happen. Stick with the situation at hand, and ask, "Why is this so unbearable? Why can't I endure it?" You'll be embarrassed to answer.

-Marcus Aurelius

When you are content to be simply yourself and don't compare or compete, everybody will respect you.

-Lao Tzu

I was gratified to be able to answer promptly, and I did.
I said I didn't know.

-Mark Twain

An angry man opens his mouth and shuts his eyes.

-Marcus Porcius Cato

> Society is well governed when its people obey the magistrates, and the magistrates obey the law.
>
> -Solon

> Silence is a source of great strength.
>
> -Lao Tzu

> It always seems impossible until it's done.
>
> -Nelson Mandela

Books constitute capital. A library book lasts as long as a house, for hundreds of years. It is not, then, an article of mere consumption but fairly of capital, and often in the case of professional men, setting out in life, it is their only capital.

-Thomas Jefferson

The higher we are placed, the more humbly we should walk.

-Marcus Tullius Cicero

It takes a great talent and skill to conceal one's talent and skill.

-La Rochefoucauld

The right word may be effective, but no word was ever as effective as a rightly timed pause.

-Mark Twain

I grow old learning something new every day.

-Solon

Do not wait; the time will never be "just right." Start where you stand, and work with whatever tools you may have at your command, and better tools will be found as you go along.

-George Herbert

Modest doubt is called the beacon of the wise.

-William Shakespeare

What it lies in our power to do, it lies in our power not to do.

-Aristotle

> If you would not be forgotten as soon as you are dead, either write something worth reading or do things worth writing.

-Benjamin Franklin

> No wealth can ever make a bad man at peace with himself.

-Plato

> All cruelty springs from weakness.

-Seneca

Talk low, talk slow, and don't say too much.

-John Wayne

I don't need a friend who changes when I change and who nods when I nod; my shadow does that much better.

-Plutarch

It is the mind - that is the mind - confusing the mind. Do not leave the mind, O mind, to the mind.

-Miyamoto Musashi

The palest ink is better than the best memory.

-Ancient Chinese Proverb

A half-truth is a whole lie

-Yiddish Proverb

How poor are they that have not patience! What wound did ever heal but by degrees?

-William Shakespeare

In the end, it's not the years in your life that count.
It's the life in your years.

-Abraham Lincoln

Whatever years be behind us are in death's hands.

-Seneca

It is not a lack of love, but a lack of friendship that makes unhappy marriages.

-Friedrich Nietzsche

You will not be punished for your anger, you will be punished by your anger.

-The Buddha

Worrying is like paying a debt you don't owe.

-Mark Twain

We make a living by what we get, but we make a life by what we give.

-Winston Churchill

Educating the mind without educating the heart is no education at all.

-Aristotle

Prove your words by your deeds.

- Seneca the Younger

The whole life of a man is but a point in time; let us enjoy it.

-Epictetus

COMPILED BY MICHAEL S. WADDINGTON

Saw the wood in front of you.

-Anonymous

True happiness is to enjoy the present without anxious dependence on the future.

-Seneca

How much easier it is to be critical than to be correct.

-Benjamin Disraeli

Do not speak of your happiness
to one less fortunate
than yourself

-Plutarch

Silence is a true friend who never betrays.

-Confucius

Believe you can and you're halfway there.

-Theodore Roosevelt

> The measure of a man is what he does with power.
>
> -Plato

> Nothing, to my way of thinking, is a better proof of a well ordered mind than a man's ability to stop just where he is and pass some time in his own company.
>
> -Marcus Aurelius

> If you find yourself in a fair fight, you didn't plan your mission properly.
>
> -Colonel David Hackworth

What man can you show me who places any value on his time, who reckons the worth of each day, who understands that he is dying daily? For we are mistaken when we look forward to death; the major portion of death has already passed.

-Seneca

Beware of little expenses. A small leak will sink a great ship.

-Benjamin Franklin

Good fences make good neighbors.

-Robert Frost

We are what we repeatedly do. Excellence, then, is not an act, but a habit. Men acquire a particular quality by constantly acting in a particular way.

-Aristotle

Fresh air impoverishes the doctor.

-Danish Proverb

He who knows best

knows how little he knows.

-Thomas Jefferson

When you have eliminated the impossible, whatever remains, however improbable, must be the truth.

-Sir Arthur Conan Doyle

To improve is to change;

to be perfect is to change often.

-Winston Churchill

The fear of death follows from the fear of life. A man who lives fully is prepared to die at any time.

-Mark Twain

If evil be spoken of you and it be true, correct yourself, if it be a lie, laugh at it.

-Epictetus

To wish to be well is a part of becoming well.

-Seneca

You can only protect your liberties in this world by protecting the other man's freedom.

-Clarence Darrow

Do what you can, with what you have, where you are.

-Theodore Roosevelt

Life is half spent before we know what it is.

-George Herbert

He who can modify his tactics in relation to his opponent and thereby succeed in winning, may be called a heaven-born captain.

-Sun Tzu

I prefer tongue-tied knowledge to ignorant loquacity.

-Marcus Tullius Cicero

Insanity is doing something over and over again and expecting a different result.

-Albert Einstein

Believe nothing, no matter where you read it, or who said it, no matter if I have said it, unless it agrees with your own reason and your own common sense.

-The Buddha

Only time can heal what reason cannot.

-Seneca

When you lose, don't lose the lesson.

-Anonymous

Wealth is not his that has it, but his that enjoys it.

-Benjamin Franklin

I have not failed. I've just found 10,000 ways that won't work.

-Thomas A. Edison

It is best to rise from life as from a banquet, neither thirsty nor drunken.

-Aristotle

Yes, you can, if you do everything as if it were the last thing you were doing in your life, and stop being aimless, stop letting your emotions override what your mind tells you, stop being hypocritical, self-centered, irritable.

-Marcus Aurelius

Nothing gives one person so much advantage over another as to remain always cool and unruffled under all circumstances.

-Thomas Jefferson

COMPILED BY MICHAEL S. WADDINGTON

They must often change who would be constant in happiness or wisdom.

-Confucius

There never was a horse that couldn't be rode; Never was a cowboy who couldn't be throwed.

-Will James

Attack him where he is unprepared, appear where you are not expected.

-Sun Tzu

To realize that you do not understand is a virtue; Not to realize that you do not understand is a defect.

-Lao Tzu

It is not that we have so little time but that we lose so much. ... The life we receive is not short but we make it so; we are not ill provided but use what we have wastefully.

-Seneca

We are masters of the unsaid words, but slaves of those we let slip out.

-Winston Churchill

Do to others what you want them to do to you.

-Matthew: 7:12

The biggest troublemaker you'll probably ever have to deal with watches you shave his face in the mirror every morning.

-Anonymous

It takes many good deeds to build a good reputation, and only one bad deed to lose it.

-Benjamin Franklin

———————

He hath no leisure who useth it not.

-George Herbert

———————

It takes time to persuade men to do even what is for their own good.

-Thomas Jefferson

Action may not always bring happiness; but there is no happiness without action.

-Benjamin Disraeli

The most important single ingredient in the formula of success is knowing how to get along with people.

-Theodore Roosevelt

The man who does not read has no advantage over the man who cannot read.

-Mark Twain

Before speaking, think twice, and then say nothing.

-Anonymous

The secret to getting ahead is getting started.

-Mark Twain

Be a craftsman in speech that thou mayest be strong, for the strength of one is the tongue, and speech is mightier than all fighting.

-Maxims of Ptahhotep

I believe that every human mind feels pleasure in doing good to another.

-Thomas Jefferson

Nothing great is created suddenly, any more than a bunch of grapes or a fig. If you tell me that you desire a fig. I answer you that there must be time. Let it first blossom, then bear fruit, then ripen.

-Epictetus

Begin at once to live, and count each separate day as a separate life.

-Seneca

Fortune sides with him who dares.

-Virgil

In war, then, let your great object be victory, not lengthy campaigns.

-Sun Tzu

When you have no basis for an argument, abuse the plaintiff.

-Marcus Tullius Cicero

A fool thinks himself to be wise, but a wise man knows himself to be a fool.

-William Shakespeare

While we wait for life, life passes.

-Seneca

A man's greatest asset is a thrifty tongue.

-Hesiod

Never piss into the wind.

-Anonymous

It is always better to have no ideas than false ones; to believe nothing, than to believe what is wrong.

-Thomas Jefferson

Whatever you are, be a good one.

-Abraham Lincoln

The easiest way to eat crow is while it's still warm. The colder it gets, the harder it is to swallow.

-Anonymous

Rudeness is a sign of weakness.

-Anonymous

Then remind yourself that past and future have no power over you. Only the present—and even that can be minimized. Just mark off its limits. And if your mind tries to claim that it can't hold out against that…well, then, heap shame upon it.

-Marcus Aurelius

Read as you taste fruit or savor wine, or enjoy friendship, love or life.

-George Herbert

COMPILED BY MICHAEL S. WADDINGTON

Three may keep a secret if two of them are dead.

-Benjamin Franklin

If money is your hope for independence, you will never have it. The only real security that a man will have in this world is a reserve of knowledge, experience, and ability.

-Henry Ford

We cannot learn men from books.

-Benjamin Disraeli

All you need in this life is ignorance and confidence; then success is sure.

-Mark Twain

Let your plans be dark and impenetrable as night, and when you move, fall like a thunderbolt.

-Sun Tzu

Do not anticipate trouble, or worry about what may never happen.

-Benjamin Franklin

I give more time to exercise of the body than of the mind, believing it wholesome to both.

-Thomas Jefferson

If you haven't fallen off a horse…then you haven't been ridi'n long enough.

- Anonymous

Wake early if you want another man's life or land. No lamb for the lazy wolf. No battles won in bed.

-Viking quote

Some people don't have much to say, but you have to listen a long time to find out.

-Mark Twain

"No comment" is a splendid expression.
I am using it again and again.

-Winston Churchill

Sometimes the best gain is to lose.

-George Herbert

If you could kick the person in the pants responsible for most of your trouble, you wouldn't sit for a month.

-Theodore Roosevelt

As long as you live,
keep learning how to live.

-Seneca

Our greatest glory is not in never falling, but in rising every time we fall.

-Confucius

Before you speak, listen. Before you write, think. Before you spend, earn. Before you invest, investigate. Before you criticize, wait. Before you pray, forgive. Before you quit, try. Before you retire, save. Before you die, give.

-William A. Ward

Life is long,
if you know how to use it.

-Seneca

The clever combatant imposes his will on the enemy, but does not allow the enemy's will to be imposed on him.

-Sun Tzu

Good words are worth much, and cost little.

-George Herbert

Adopt the pace of nature: her secret is patience.

-Ralph Waldo Emerson

Today I escaped from anxiety. Or no, I discarded it, because it was within me, in my own perceptions - not outside.

-Marcus Aurelius

The best way to keep good acts in memory is to refresh them with new.

-Marcus Porcius Cato

There's one way to find out if a man is honest: ask him; if he says yes, you know he's crooked.

-Mark Twain

Because power corrupts, society's demands for moral authority and character increase as the importance of the position increases.

-John Adams

Twenty years from now you will be more disappointed by the things you didn't do than by the ones you did do. So throw off the bowlines. Sail away from the safe harbor. Catch the trade winds in your sails. Explore. Dream. Discover.

-Mark Twain

Be wary of the man who urges an action in which he himself incurs no risk.

-Joaquín Setantí

I am a great believer in luck, and I find the harder I work, the more I have of it.

- Thomas Jefferson

Only the educated are free.

-Epictetus

ABOUT THE EDITOR

Michael Waddington is a criminal defense lawyer who has successfully defended cases in military courtrooms around the world, including Japan, South Korea, Germany, Iraq, Bahrain, Italy, England, and across the United States. He's been involved in some of the highest profile court martial cases and has been reported on and quoted by hundreds of major media sources worldwide.

He is also the best-selling author of The Art of Trial Warfare: Winning at Trial Using Sun Tzu's The Art of War. He has provided consultation services to CNN, 60 Minutes, ABC Nightline, the BBC, CBS, and the Golden Globe winning TV series, "The Good Wife." He appeared in a major CNN Documentary, 2009's "Killings at the Canal," and some of his cases have been the subject of books and movies, including the Academy Award Winning Documentary "Taxi to the Dark Side," and the 2013 documentary, "The Kill Team."

He is the creator of the *Trial Warrior Boot Camp*, an intensive trial advocacy course that teaches lawyers battle proven trail tactics and strategies on a condensed time table.

Since 2013, he has been an annual contributor to the American Bar Association's publication, "The State of Criminal Justice." He is also a fellow of the American Board of Criminal Lawyers (ABCL).

www.ingramcontent.com/pod-product-compliance
Lightning Source LLC
Chambersburg PA
CBHW061436180526
45170CB00004B/1440